Stock Cars (Horsepower)

Matt Doeden
AR B.L.: 2.7
Points: 0.5   MG

BLAZERS

HORSEPOWER

STOCK CARS

by Matt Doeden

Reading Consultant:

Barbara J. Fox

Reading Specialist

North Carolina State University

Capstone press

Mankato, Minnesota

Blazers is published by Capstone Press,
151 Good Counsel Drive, P.O. Box 669, Mankato, Minnesota 56002.
www.capstonepress.com

Library of Congress Cataloging-in-Publication Data
Doeden, Matt.
    Stock cars / by Matt Doeden.
      p. cm.—(Blazers. Horsepower)
    Includes bibliographical references and index.
    ISBN 0-7368-3792-2 (hardcover)
    ISBN 0-7368-5215-8 (paperback)
    1. Stock car racing—United States—Juvenile literature.
    I. Title. II. Series.
GV1029.9.S74D66 2005
796.72—dc22   2004018532

Summary: Discusses stock cars, their main features, and how they are raced.

Editorial Credits
Erika L. Shores, editor; Jason Knudson, set designer; Patrick D. Dentinger, book designer; Wanda Winch, photo researcher; Scott Thoms, photo editor

Photo Credits
Getty Images Inc./Chris Stanford, cover, 18–19; Darrell Ingham, 24–25; Jonathan Ferrey, 20–21; Robert Laberge, 26, 27
SportsChrome Inc., 12–13, 14–15, 16–17; Brian Spurlock, 22–23, 28–29 Greg Crisp, 10–11
Zuma Press/Karl Larsen, 8, 9; Larry Burton – KPA, 4–5, 6–7

1 2 3 4 5 6 10 09 08 07 06 05

TABLE OF CONTENTS

STOCK CARS

The roar of engines fills the air as 43 stock cars begin a race. Matt Kenseth's number 17 car starts in the middle of the pack.

Kenseth fights his way through traffic. He speeds into a turn, passes a car, and takes the lead.

Kenseth pulls away from the pack. The checkered flag waves as he crosses the finish line and wins the race.

9

STOCK CAR DESIGN

Stock cars have the same shape as cars built in a factory. But all of the stock car parts are built just for racing.

Stock cars look different than
regular cars on the inside. Stock cars
have only one seat. A driver sees
many gauges on the dashboard.

BLAZER FACT

Drivers often follow closely
behind another car. This
strategy is called drafting. It
helps the cars go faster.

Gauges

Stock cars do not have doors.
Drivers get in and out through
the window.

Built for Speed

Stock cars have powerful eight-cylinder engines. The cars can go more than 200 miles (320 kilometers) per hour.

Smooth tires called slicks help stock cars grip the track. Slicks wear down during a race. Crews change the slicks during pit stops.

A good pit stop takes only about 15 seconds.

STOCK CAR DIAGRAM

Slick tire

Air dam

Spoiler

STOCK CARS IN ACTION

NASCAR's Nextel Cup is the biggest stock car series. Nextel Cup races can be as long as 600 miles (966 kilometers).

Racing teams pay attention to safety. Drivers wear helmets and fireproof racing suits. Strong seat belts hold drivers tightly in place.

Cars are built to protect drivers during crashes. Drivers usually walk away from even the worst crashes.

STOCK CARS SPEED AROUND THE TRACK!

GLOSSARY

cylinder (SIL-uhn-dur)—a hollow area inside an engine in which fuel burns to create power

dashboard (DASH-bord)—the instrument panel of a car or truck

factory (FAK-tuh-ree)—the place where a product, such as a car, is made

gauge (GAYJ)—a dial or instrument used to measure something, such as an engine's temperature

pack (PACK)—a group of cars in a race

series (SIHR-eez)—a group of races that make up one season; drivers earn points for finishing races in a series.

slicks (SLIKS)—tires that have no tread

READ MORE

Dubois, Muriel L. *Pro Stock Cars.* Wild Rides! Mankato, Minn.: Capstone Press, 2002.

Gigliotti, Jim. *Fantastic Finishes: NASCAR's Great Races.* The World of NASCAR. Chanhassen, Minn.: Child's World, 2004.

Maurer, Tracy. *Stock Cars.* Roaring Rides. Vero Beach, Fla.: Rourke, 2004.

INTERNET SITES

FactHound offers a safe, fun way to find Internet sites related to this book. All of the sites on FactHound have been researched by our staff.

Here's how:

1. Visit *www.facthound.com*
2. Type in this special code **0736837922** for age-appropriate sites. Or, enter a search word related to this book for a more general search.
3. Click on the **Fetch It** button.

FactHound will fetch the best sites for you!

INDEX